Viol.I.
Viol.II.
Viola.
Vell.I.
Vell.II.
Bass.
sempre p
pp
sf
Ob.
Clar.
Fag.
Corni in C.
mf
p
cresc.

8   Overture to *The Bartered Bride*

10   Overture to *The Bartered Bride*

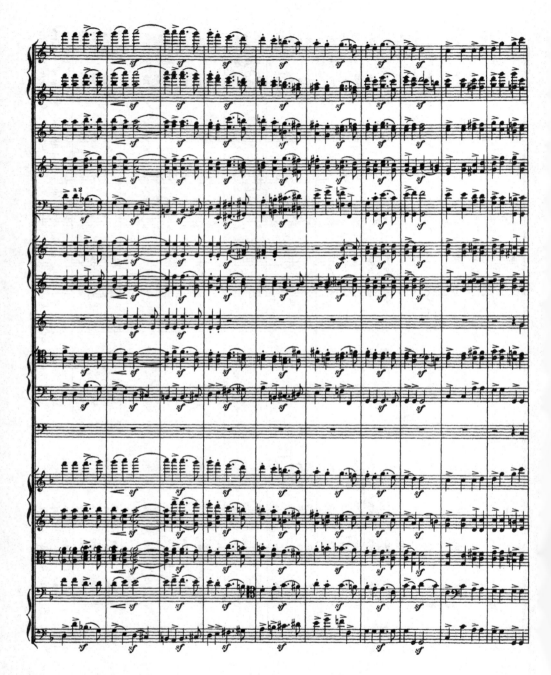

20   Overture to *The Bartered Bride*

Overture to *The Bartered Bride*

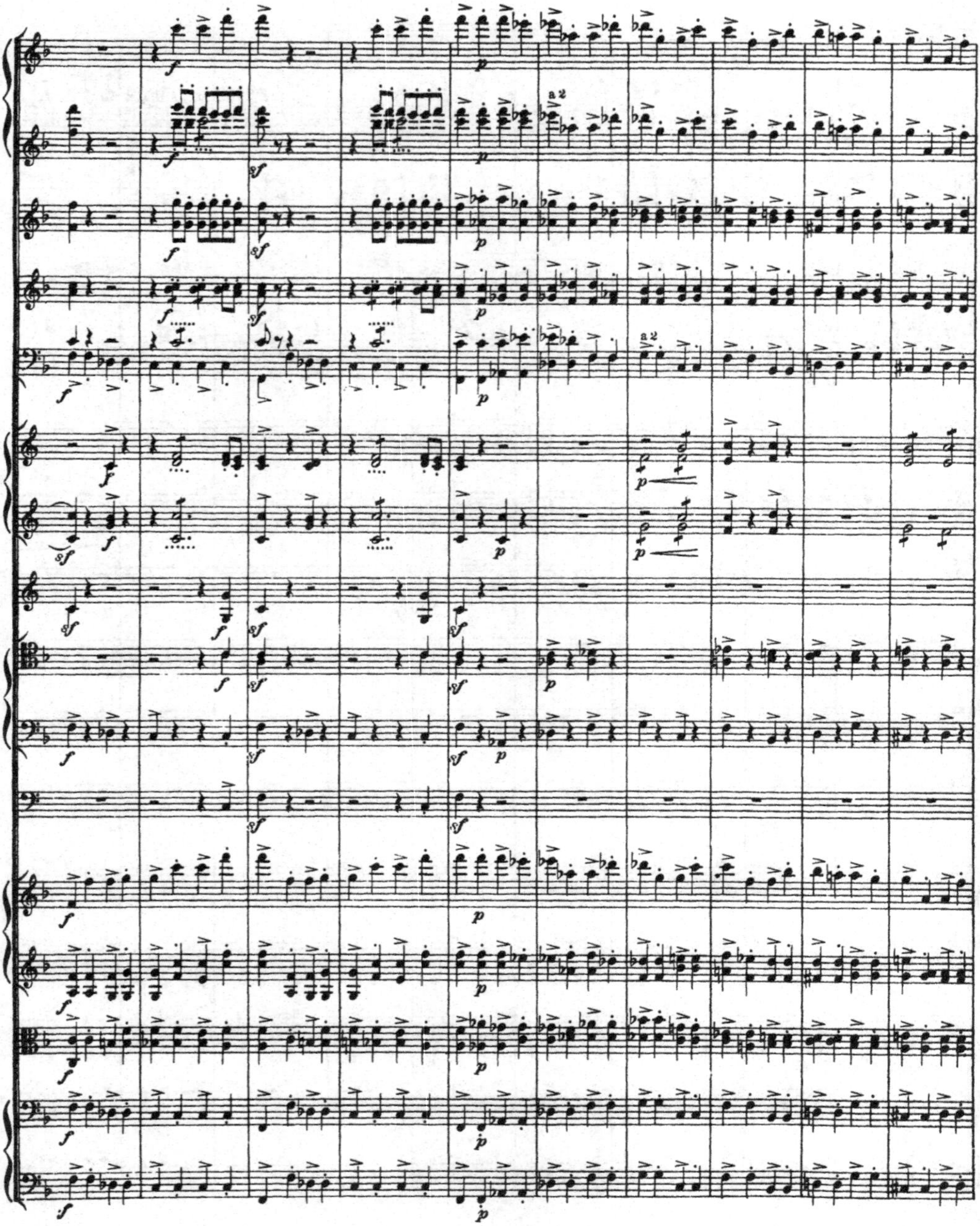
a 2
a 2

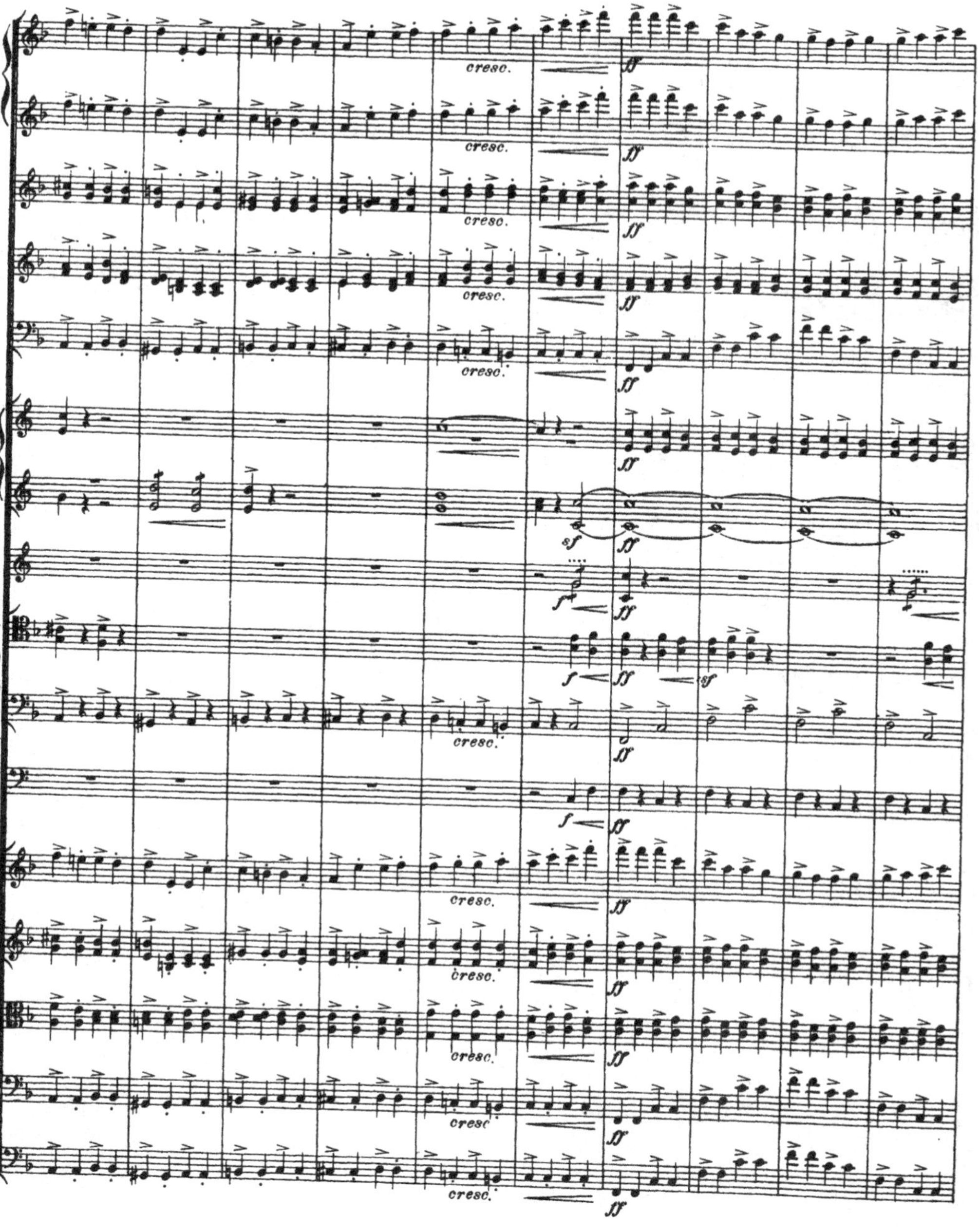
cresc.
ff
sf
f

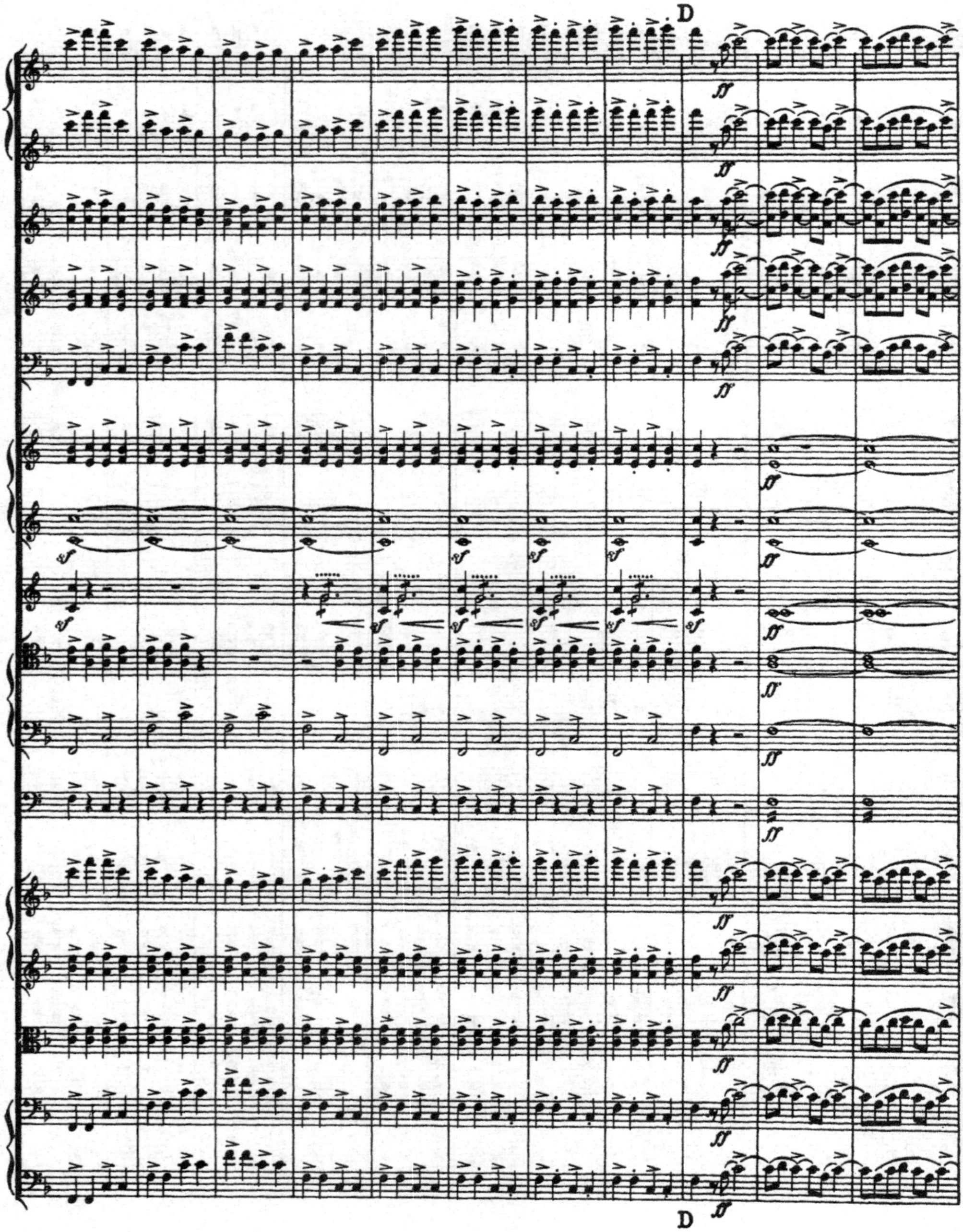
D
D

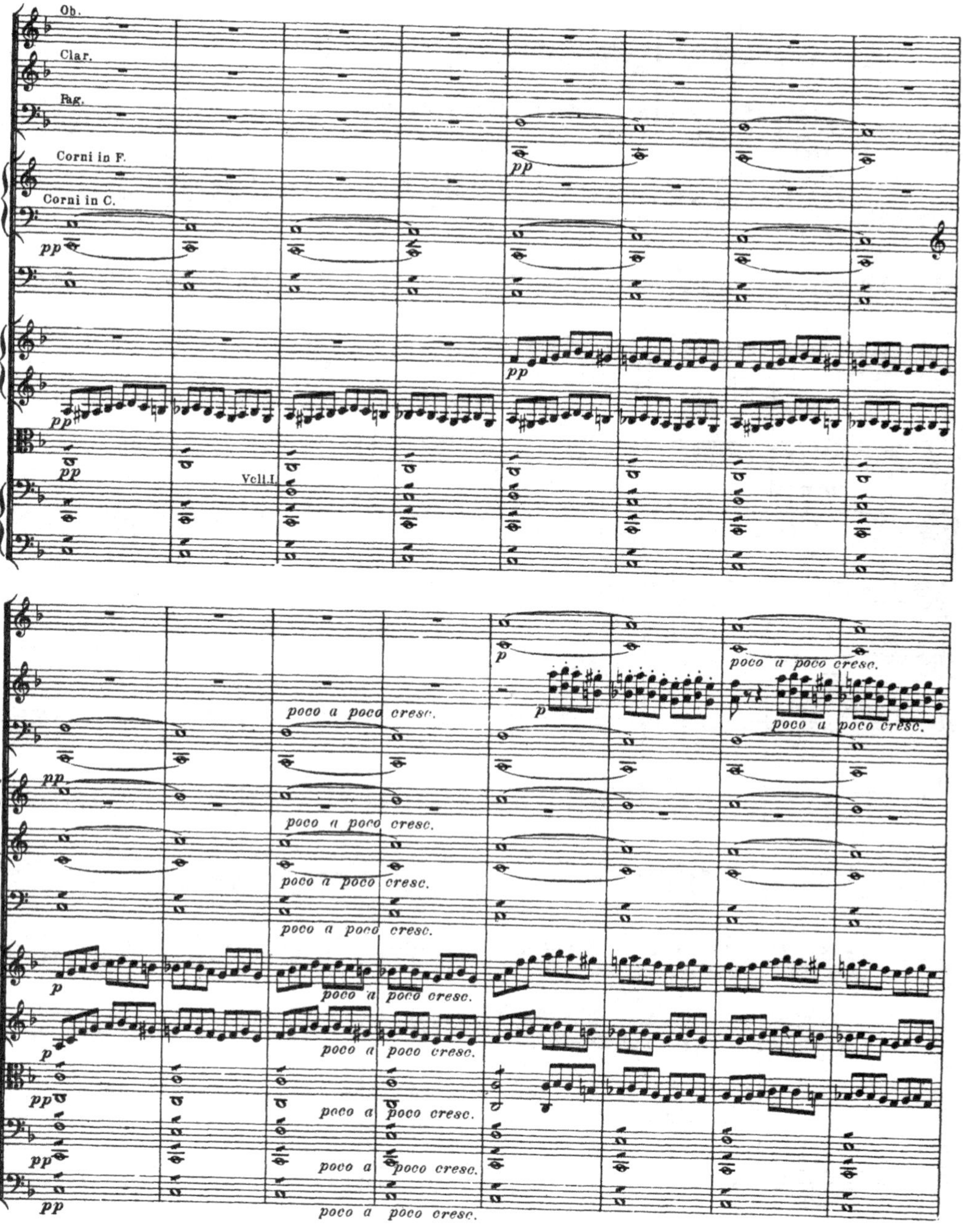
Ob.
Clar.
Fag.
Corni in F.
Corni in C.
pp
Vcll.I.
p
poco a poco cresc.

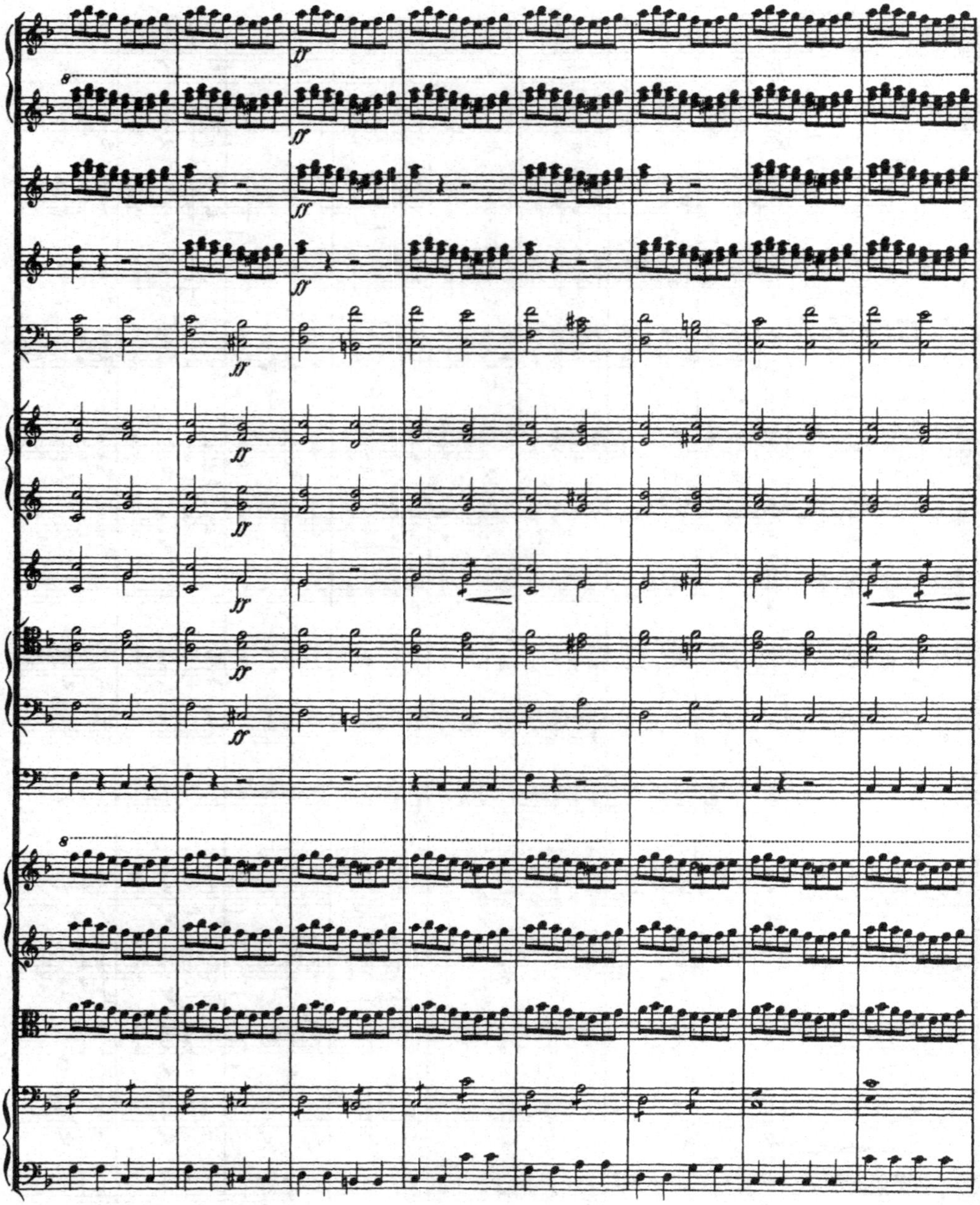
ff

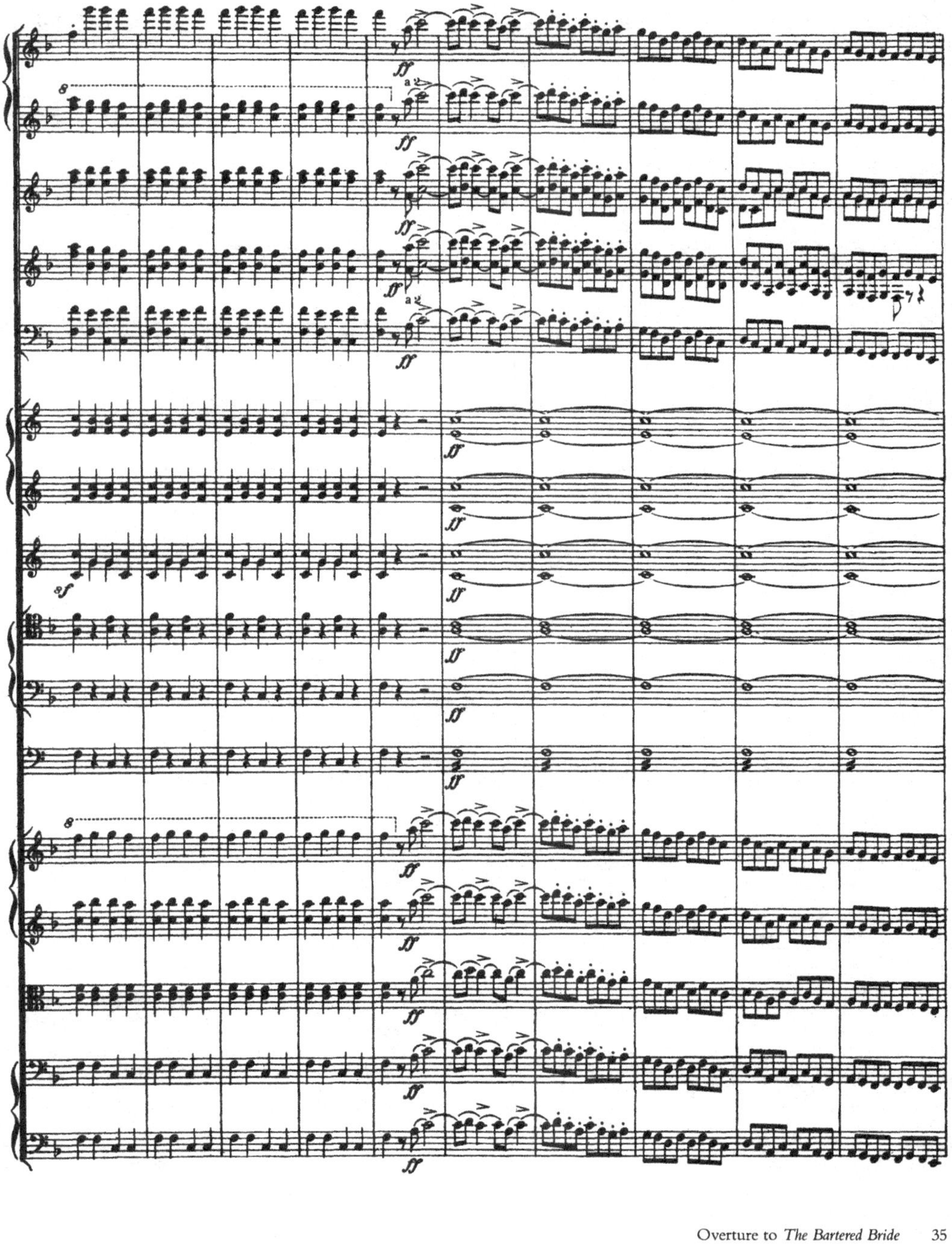

a 2
a 2

"Polka"

from the opera *The Bartered Bride*

40   "Polka" from *The Bartered Bride*

1395

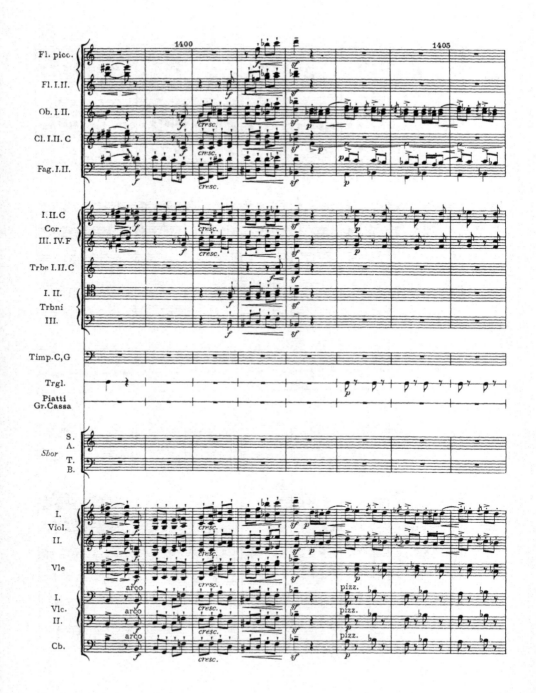

44   "Polka" from *The Bartered Bride*

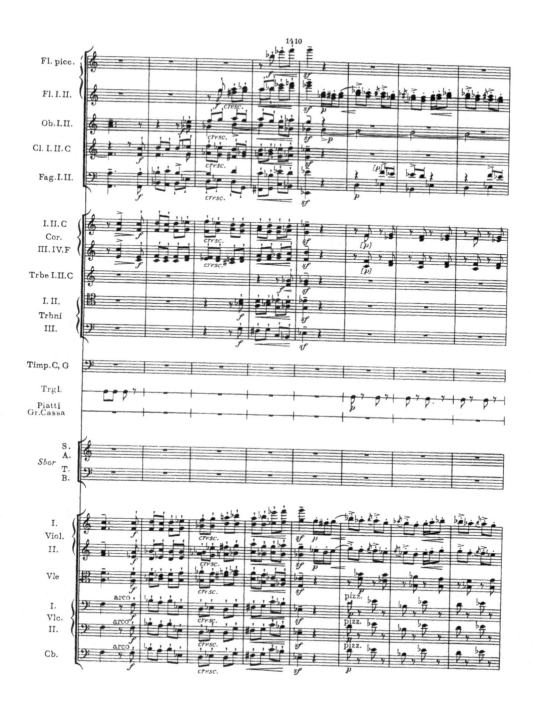

"Polka" from *The Bartered Bride*

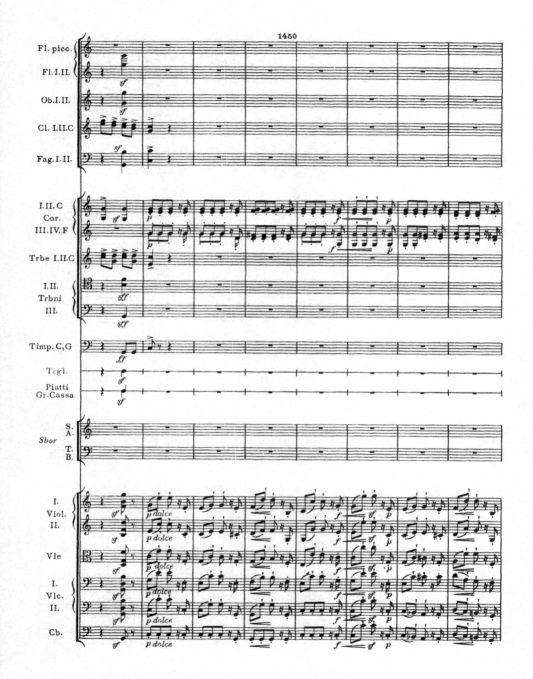

"Polka" from *The Bartered Bride*

"Polka" from *The Bartered Bride*

"Polka" from *The Bartered Bride*

58   "Polka" from *The Bartered Bride*

Ru-ka v ru-ce, hle-dy v hled: s ná-mi toč se   ce-lý svět!

"Polka" from *The Bartered Bride*

"Polka" from *The Bartered Bride*

"Polka" from *The Bartered Bride*

"Polka" from *The Bartered Bride*

"Polka" from *The Bartered Bride*

"Furiant"

from the opera *The Bartered Bride*

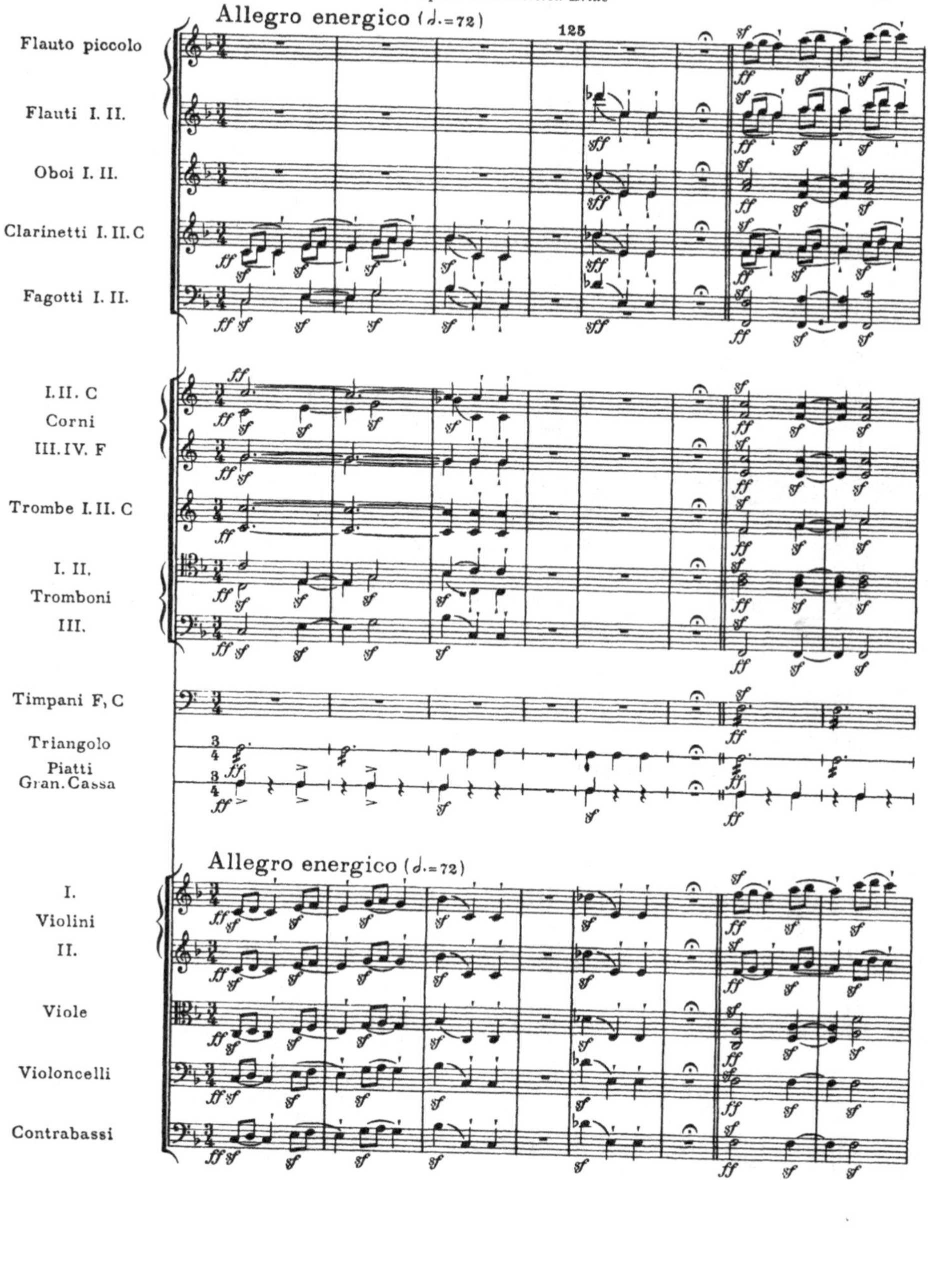

"Furiant" from *The Bartered Bride*

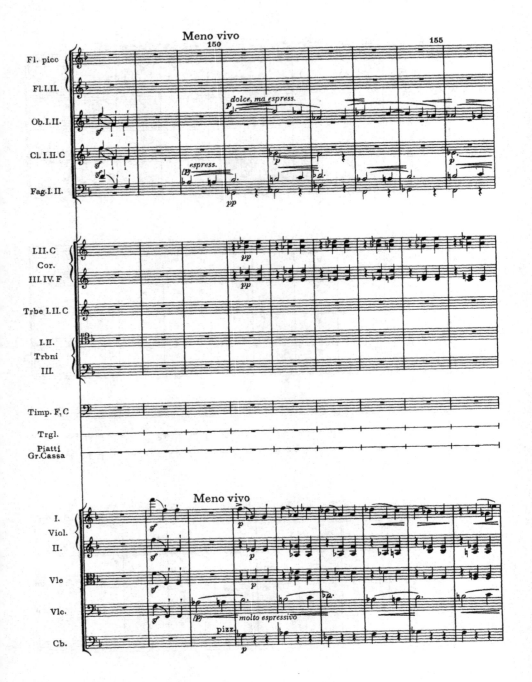

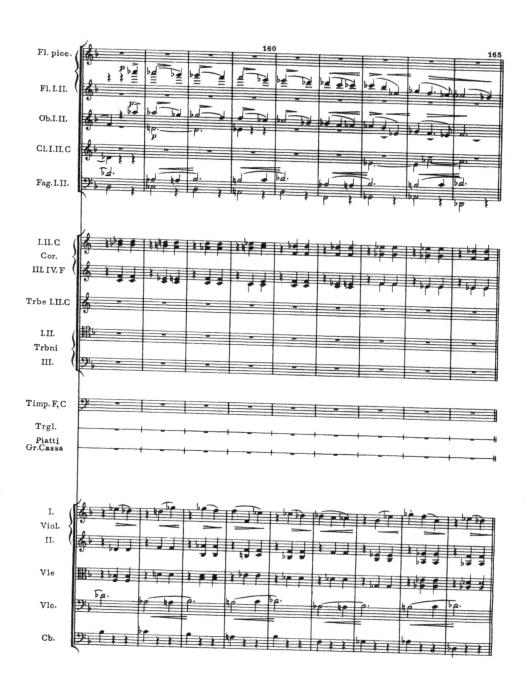

76   "Furiant" from *The Bartered Bride*

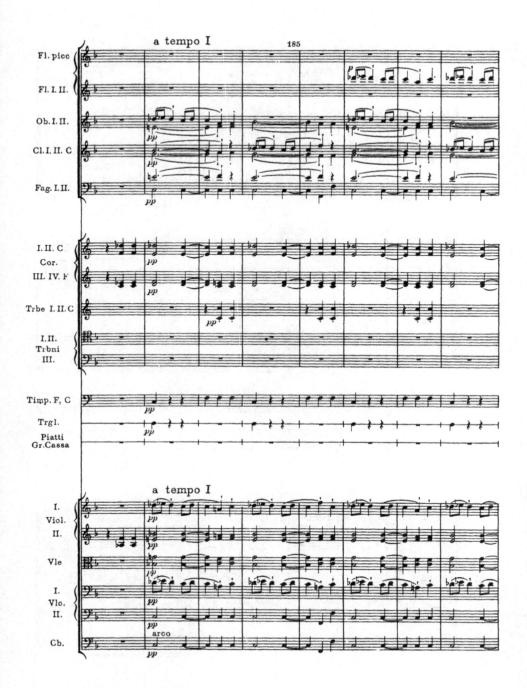

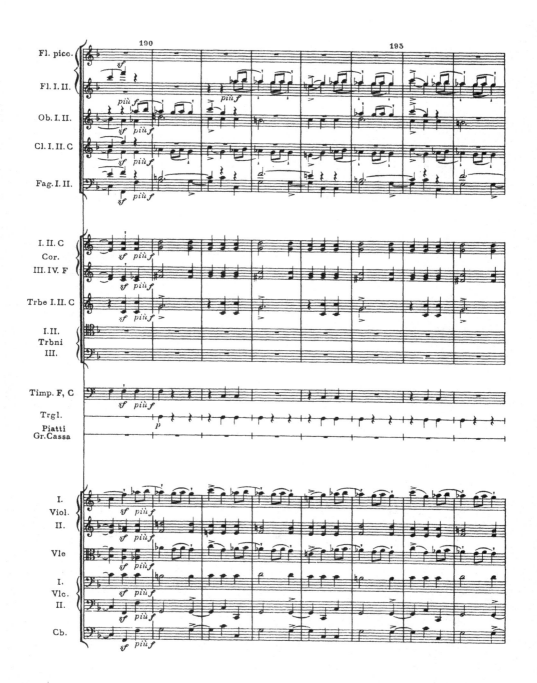

82   "Furiant" from *The Bartered Bride*

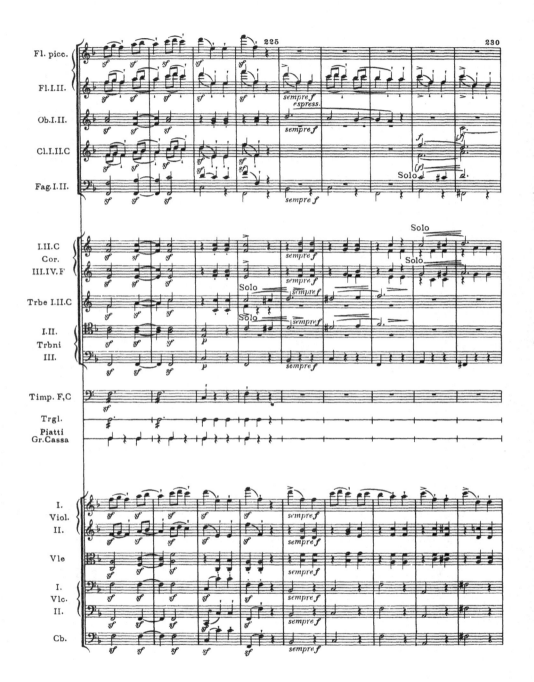

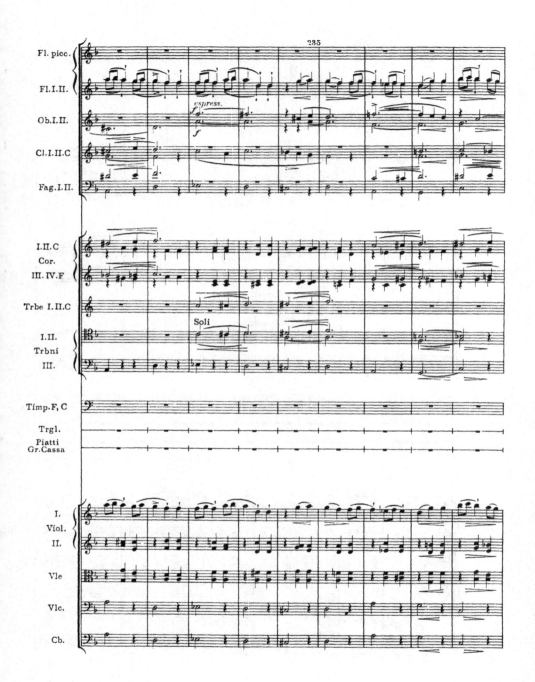

84   "Furiant" from *The Bartered Bride*

86   "Furiant" from *The Bartered Bride*

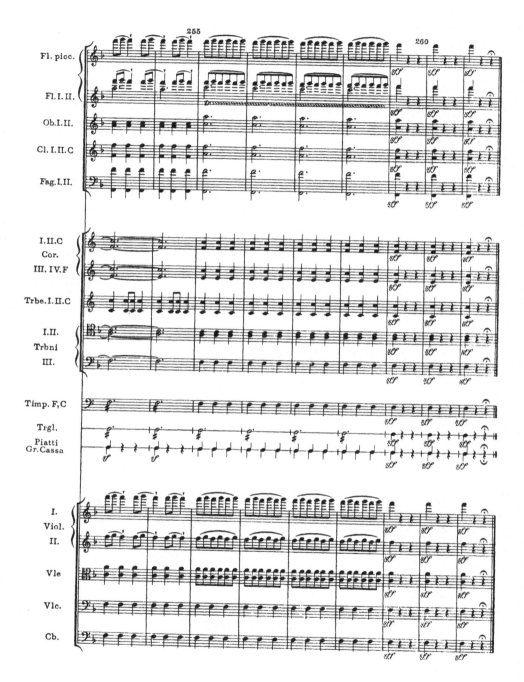

"Dance of the Comedians"

from the opera *The Bartered Bride*

90   "Dance of the Comedians" from *The Bartered Bride*

"Dance of the Comedians" from *The Bartered Bride*

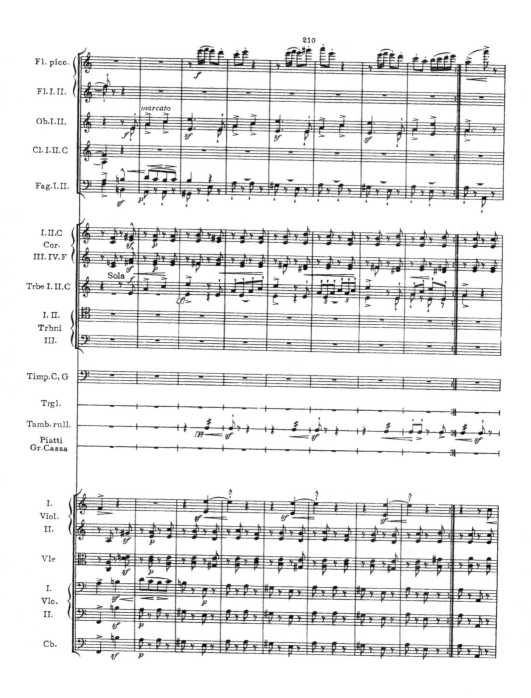

"Dance of the Comedians" from *The Bartered Bride*   97

"Dance of the Comedians" from *The Bartered Bride*

100   "Dance of the Comedians" from *The Bartered Bride*

"Dance of the Comedians" from *The Bartered Bride*   101

"Dance of the Comedians" from *The Bartered Bride*

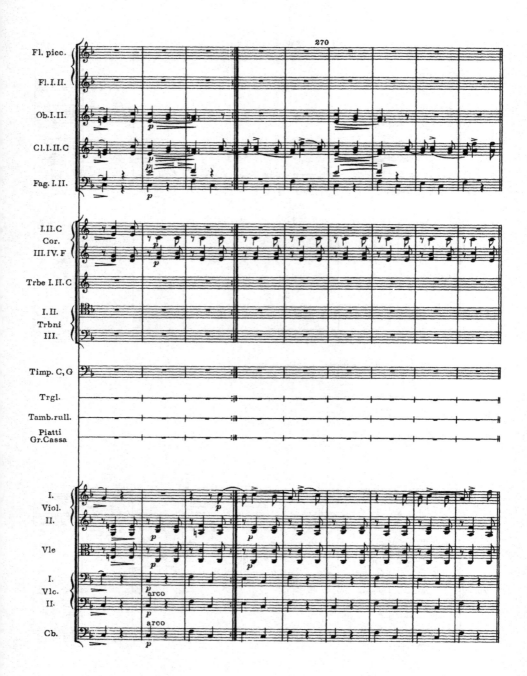

"Dance of the Comedians" from *The Bartered Bride*

106 "Dance of the Comedians" from *The Bartered Bride*

108   "Dance of the Comedians" from *The Bartered Bride*

"Dance of the Comedians" from *The Bartered Bride*   109

"Dance of the Comedians" from *The Bartered Bride*

"Dance of the Comedians" from *The Bartered Bride*　　111

"Dance of the Comedians" from *The Bartered Bride*

"Dance of the Comedians" from *The Bartered Bride*

"Dance of the Comedians" from *The Bartered Bride*

118 "Dance of the Comedians" from *The Bartered Bride*

120   "Dance of the Comedians" from *The Bartered Bride*

"Dance of the Comedians" from *The Bartered Bride*   121

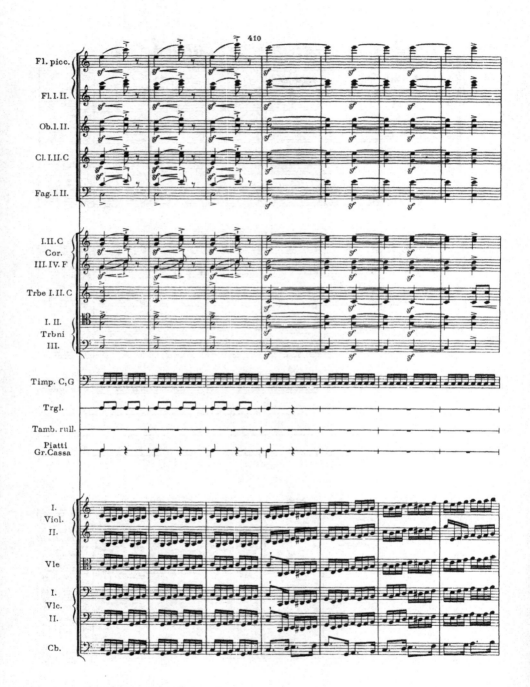

"Dance of the Comedians" from *The Bartered Bride*

"Dance of the Comedians" from *The Bartered Bride*   123

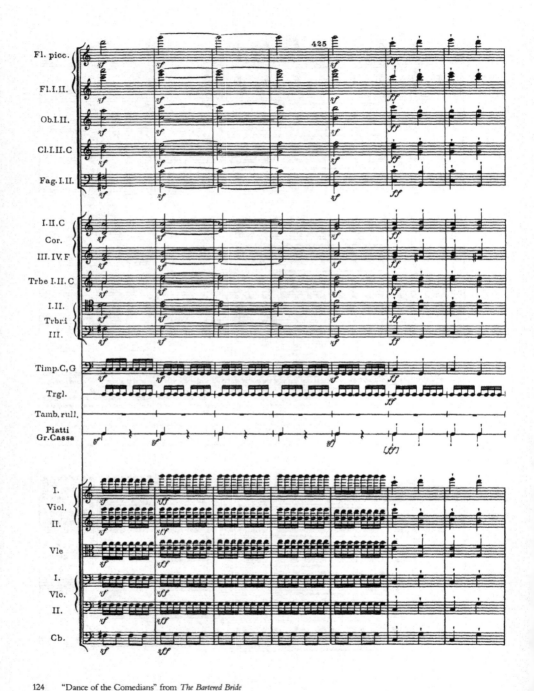

"Dance of the Comedians" from *The Bartered Bride*

Two symphonic poems from

MY FATHERLAND
Má vlast

A cycle of symphonic poems

"The Moldau" • *Vltava*
"From Bohemian Fields and Groves" • *Z českých luhů a hajů*

INSTRUMENTATION

[Names and terms are in German in the score of "The Moldau," but in Italian in "From Bohemian Fields and Groves." Both languages are represented in the bracketed instrument names below.

In this edition of "The Moldau," passages marked with an asterisk—usually written in small notes—are possible substitute orchestrations for smaller ensembles.]

Piccolo [kleine Flöte, Kl. Fl. / Flauto piccolo, Fl. picc.]
2 Flutes [Flöten, Fl. / Flauti]
2 Oboes [Oboen, Ob. / Oboi]
2 Clarinets in C, A, Bb ("B") [Klarinetten, Klar. / Clarinetti, Clar., Cl.]
2 Bassoons [Fagotte, Fag. / Fagotti]

4 Horns in C, Eb ("Es"), E, F, G, Bb ("B")–basso [Hörner, Hr. / Corni, Cor.]
2 Trumpets in C, D, E, G, Bb ("B") [Trompeten, Trpt. / Trombe, Tr.]
3 Trombones [Posaunen, Pos. / Trombone, Trb.]
Tuba [Tuba]

Timpani [Pauken, Pk. / Timpani, Timp.]

Percussion
    Triangle [Triangel, Trgl. / Triangolo]
    Bass Drum & Cymbals [Große Trommel (Gr. Tr.) und Becken (Bck.) / Piatti]

Harp (or Piano) [Harfe (oder Klavier)]

Violins I & II [Violine/o, Viol.]
Violas [Bratsche, Br. / Viola]
Cellos [Violoncell(o), Vcll(o)]
Basses [Kontrabaß, K.-B. / Contrabasso, C.-B.]

"The Moldau"

Vltava

Symphonic poem from the cycle *My Fatherland*

The Two Sources of the Moldau

130   "The Moldau"

40

136   "The Moldau"

Forest Hunt

Peasant Wedding

"The Moldau"

"The Moldau"

261

168   "The Moldau"

266

309

328

The Moldau in its Greatest Breadth

333 Più moto

350

"The Moldau"   183

Vyšehrad Motive (Symphonic Poem No. 1)

"The Moldau"

392

"From Bohemian Fields and Groves"

Z českých luhů a hajů

Symphonic poem from the cycle *My Fatherland*

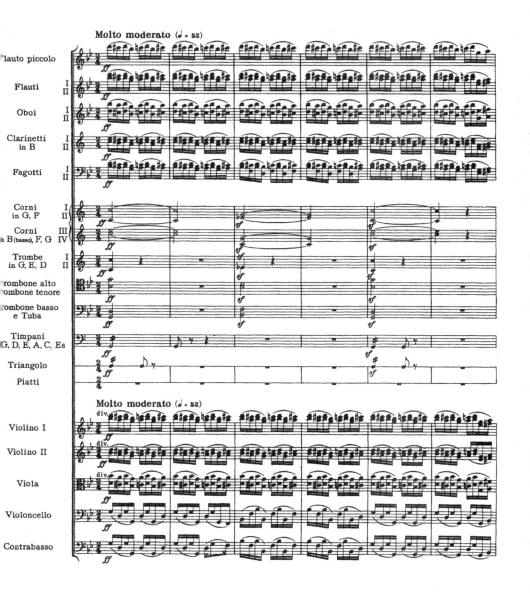

194   "From Bohemian Fields and Groves"

"From Bohemian Fields and Groves"

"From Bohemian Fields and Groves"

200   "From Bohemian Fields and Groves"

"From Bohemian Fields and Groves"

"From Bohemian Fields and Groves"

"From Bohemian Fields and Groves"

"From Bohemian Fields and Groves"

220

"From Bohemian Fields and Groves"

275

299

222   "From Bohemian Fields and Groves"

"From Bohemian Fields and Groves"

346

"From Bohemian Fields and Groves"

"From Bohemian Fields and Groves"

380

387

"From Bohemian Fields and Groves"

"From Bohemian Fields and Groves"

"From Bohemian Fields and Groves"

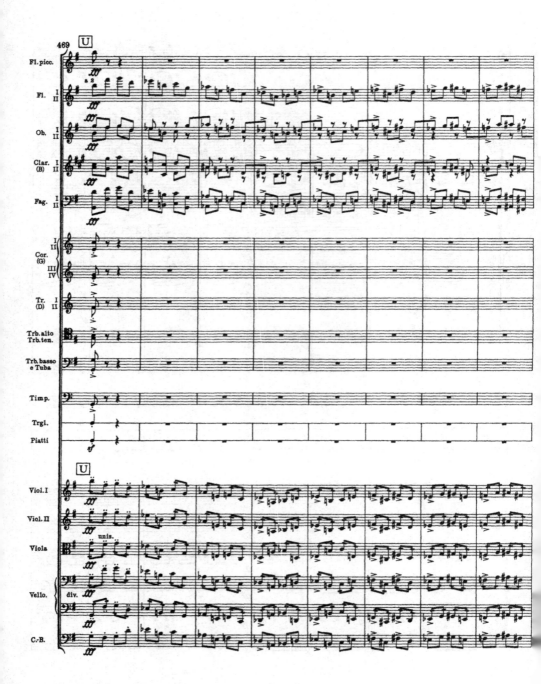

485

"From Bohemian Fields and Groves"

"From Bohemian Fields and Groves"

521

"From Bohemian Fields and Groves"

580

"From Bohemian Fields and Groves"

END OF EDITION